CAMPAIGN-O-MATIC!

How Small Businesses Build Big Ad Campaigns

Johnny Molson

Andover

For Patton and Paul who started it all.
And for Emily and Annelise who make sure I don't stop.

Contents

INTRODUCTION

You are not a small business. As my friend and business partner Tim Miles aptly points out, there is nothing small about what you do every day. You've put it all on the line. Your family is counting on you, and the families of your employees are counting on you. Just because you're not Nike, Proctor & Gamble, or McDonald's doesn't mean you can't have a solid, cohesive ad campaign. Just because Madison Avenue won't take your call, is no reason your local company can't make a stand in your town and profit like royalty. I love local businesses. I absolutely love seeing them grow and thrive.

No matter how many Amazons, WalMarts, or Costcos come, your kitchen-table company will always have a place. By applying marketing principles, local businesses not only win...they soar.

Businesses get an average of 16 different sales people each month, all doing their Professor Harold Hill song-and-dance and telling you *their* advertising elixir is better than the other guy's. I believe success means more than one good ad (or advertising vehicle). I believe by being laser-consistent and deftly-different, you win. Bounce around like a hundred ping-pong balls, you lose.

This book is for you. And although we haven't met, I think you're doing something amazing. As far as I'm concerned, you're already Big Business.

PART ONE
INFO GATHERING

CHAPTER 1

LOOK OUTSIDE

In the Fall of 2012, Wentworth Plumbing was in a position many plumbers find themselves in. In a city of about 225,000, Jim Wentworth was up against 13 legitimate plumbing companies and another 28 dudes with a truck and a wrench. Being one of the 13 is competitive enough. Slogging it out with a bunch of greasy one-man operations who can (and do) charge anything was clearly eating into his profits... And patience.

"I have almost twice the experience of those guys!"

"I know you do, Jim."

"They don't even use industry parts. They get them from Home Depot."

This is where we had to slide back a step or three. Wentworth found himself in a labyrinth of *logical justification.* Each legitimate point he felt he had either fell under the category of "nobody cares," or was not remarkable enough to make a profound difference. It wasn't easy for him to swallow, but looking honestly and objectively, it appeared that all the plumbers in town were pretty much the same.

If you remove the goggles of pride you have on for your business, you will likely find your competitors are plenty competent and capable. Occasionally, clear differences like the ones between Sack's Fifth Avenue and Walmart make a marketer's job easy. Usually, it's just varying shades of Target.

Advertising is the "public face" of your business. It's how customers know you *before* they *know* you. It also gives you an easy (and free) bit of intel about what your *competitors* are doing. You can choose to harvest the field that has twelve other tractors (and hope your tractor is a bit faster and has more gas), or you can look west and find a field you can have all to yourself. The law of Market Positioning says you are wise to find your own field.

Jim Wentworth's first task was to list the things his competitors were saying in their advertising. He set out to investigate what they were putting out there, so he could understand what words and positions were already taken. Here's what Jim found:

ROMANO PLUMB, → REMODELING
SPEEDY PLUMB, → 24/7 EMERGENCY
CANNING & SONS → COMMERCIAL &
                  NEW CONST.

MARK ROBINSON HVAC & PLM → DUCT CLEANING

The remaining plumbers were either doing no major advertising or had no discernable position in the market. This was good news for a company like Wentworth's. Only a handful of market positions had been claimed. The rest of the competition had no defined position.

 **Market Position** – The category or "position" your company has in the minds of consumers. It's what you are "known for." Tiffany's is "known for" high-end luxury jewelry. Costco is "known for" warehouse bulk products at low prices. Enterprise Rent-A-Car is "known for" bringing your rental car to you.

Below, list your main competitors and what they are known for:

CHAPTER 2

WHAT DO THEY WANT?

"What don't you get, Josh?"

"Well, there's a million robots that turn into something. And, this is a building that turns into a robot. So, what's fun about playing with a building? That's not any fun."

–BIG, Twentieth Century Fox

When Josh Baskin unintentionally emasculates his buttoned-up foe in the 1988 movie *BIG*, an important marketing lesson is learned: Listening to the customer is the most reliable research you will ever do. This is not the same thing as "the customer is always right." Think of it more like convenient breadcrumbs the customer is leaving for you.

"Tell me again how you did this?"

"Well, see, it was kinda like this. People'd call and be like 'How much for 3 rooms?' and I told 'em 'That's not how it's done, I gotta come out and measure. And they'd be like 'Can't you just give me an estimate?' and I'd say 'Noooo, darlin'."

Sue-Ann wasn't terribly good at "cutting-to-the-chase." This went on for another 15 minutes until she finally got to the bullseye:

"So, I talked to my customers, and they said that they wished I could just give them a flat rate. So I did."

"That's it?"

"That's it."

"That's goddamn brilliant."

Sue-Ann's house cleaning company was up against national franchises, competitors with bigger budgets, and she had little money for advertising.

When you need someone to clean your house, the industry standard is to go through the laborious task of setting an appointment, taking time off work, and hoping the price is right...otherwise, you start all over.

Most of the homes Sue-Ann cleans are about 3500 square feet. 70% of her clients are in a 15-20 mile radius. The median size of a home in that radius is 3000 square feet.

"I made an ad that said 'We'll clean 4 rooms, any size, $149.' Boom."

"Didn't you lose money?"

"Of course. There's one place over on Tennison Drive that's more than 6200 square feet. But I got 2 of 'em that are only 2300 square feet. See what I'm gettin' at?"

Boom. What she's getting at is that she eliminated one of the big hurdles in hiring a cleaning service. When you call to get a price, she is able to give you a price. Right now.

This idea came about from an ad-hoc focus group Sue-Ann put together. She invited 10 of her best customers to come to her place for a pot luck. She asked questions, took notes, asked more questions, and took more notes. She didn't challenge any of the ideas. She just listened. Business schools call this being "market oriented."

 **Market Orientation** – The act of looking at your company from the customer's perspective. Warning: Don't try to do this yourself. You are too close to your company to ever see it as your customers see it. You **must** talk to them.

Conducting market research isn't overly complicated, and it doesn't have to be expensive. A customer survey using a (mostly) free service like SurveyMonkey can suffice. Focus groups are easy to put together, and contrary to conventional wisdom, you don't need an independent moderator. You can do it yourself. The most important thing is what Sue-Ann knew instinctively: Listen. Don't judge. Don't argue. Don't explain why an idea won't work. Just listen.

This kind of fuzzy information, or "qualitative data," gives you an eagle's eye view of what's going on. You are trying to learn what frustrates your customers, what excites them, and how you can help them better.

It's important to note that it is not an exact science. You are hoping to find some useful insight, but don't assume that just because a few people said it, everyone else feels that way too. You are trying to get guidance. Sue-Ann learned that there was something keeping people from doing business with her, and she found a way to remove it entirely from the picture.

"I got a call from one of those guys at Nickels. He was

furious and said I was using 'unfair tactics' and 'going against industry standards'!"

"People don't like it when others have good ideas, Sue-Ann. What did you say?"

"I said thanks for the six customers who stopped using you and came to me!"

"Don't find customers for your products. Find products for your customer."

— Seth Godin

CHAPTER 3

CHOOSE WHO OVER WHAT

Charlie Lenz is the picture of "the millionaire next door." Grease and dirt had taken up residence under his fingernails and never seemed to leave. Even on Sunday-go-to-meetin', he appeared unkempt. But his HVAC business is run with precision learned from his time in the Navy.

"Lemme show you something." Charlie produced a manila folder, which had turned the same color as his fingernails.

"Looks like you've been doing some surveys."

"Every customer. Don't care if it's a repair job or a new

install. Now, check this out: 32% of my customers are between 25 and 44. 28% of my customers are between 45 and 64. That's it. That's the bullseye. We have to talk to those people between 35 and 45. Don't even talk to me about that rock radio station. Where are the Moms and business people?"

"So 60% of your customers are between 25 and 64?"

"Right."

"I know exactly where those people are." For dramatic effect, I begin a staring contest with Charlie, hoping he will answer his own question.

"Well? Where?" he barked.

"Everywhere."

Those ratios he found are almost *identical* to the ratios of the U.S. population. His customers were...average. Business owners don't like to admit this, because it sounds like they aren't special. But in fact, most of his customers are that age because *most of the population* **is** that age.

"Where are they?"

"Who?"

"Those people! 24 to 64!"

"I asked you 'who'."

"24- to 64-year-olds!!"

"Those are *whats*. **Who** is your customer?"

"Who?"

Before we get dangerously close to slipping into an Abbot and Costello routine, allow me to clarify this key difference: **Demographics** only tell you "what" a person is (male, female, age, etc.). Knowing "who" the customers are allows you to speak to them in their language about what is important to them. This information doesn't exist in demographics. Age doesn't determine a person's values or lifestyles. Charlie needs to think less about demographics and more about *psychographics* – A fancy way to say "what's going on in the noggin?"

"You believe your customers are Moms and business people?"

"Yes. Those are the people with the money. College kids don't have money. Senior citizens all use Gramanski 'cuz he's been around since Jesus."

"What do your customers all have in common besides age?"

Exasperated by these questions, he said, "I don't know, man. They all have houses that are..."

"STOP!"

Here's the point: Age isn't telling you much about anything. But looking at their minds and hearts, you can begin to discover a few things. Charlie's customers are homeowners. Now, it doesn't take an MBA to deduce that, but it's the answer he needs. A 28-year-old homeowner and a 49-year-old homeowner are his customers. They have an HVAC, and it's going to need service someday. Female or male, they both want their homes to be comfortable.

It's tempting (and too easy) to over-engineer this. You try to find the "perfect" customer, and then try to replicate her "demographic" twin. But you'll soon discover that you've gone so narrow that you have unintentionally eliminated legitimate customers. If you're a dentist, find someone with a mouth. If you're a restaurant, talk to people who have stomachs and are hungry.

Proctor and Gamble's Chief Marketing Officer Marc Pritchard, a guy who spends over $7 billion of P&G's money on marketing, discovered this while advertising Febreze. Using targeted Facebook ads, Febreze advertised specifically to large families and people with pets. Not a bad idea, since both segments are likely to have a stinky house. But Pritchard discovered that by doing this, he was ignoring too many people. Febreze's customers are people with *noses*. If you have a nose and $4.98 in your pocket, you need to know about Febreze. When Pritchard expanded to include "all nose-having adults," sales went up. "We targeted too much, and we went too narrow," he said in a Wall Street Journal interview.

Understanding *who* your customer is will always be more valuable than knowing *what* your customer is.

 **Demographics** – Raw data about a population of people. Demographics seeks to log information such as gender, age, marital status, income, zip code, education level, and race. Think of demographics as the information you leave on a census.

Psychographics – Information about one's values, attitudes, opinions, and interests. It can cover endless aspects of people. What do you like or don't like? What is relaxing for you? What issues keep you up at night? How do you feel about people who put ketchup on hotdogs? Psychographics is looking for traits of a person's character.

Firmographics – If you sell business to business, your version of psychographics is called firmographics. Like psychographics, you are looking for deeper information than "how many employees" or "annual gross profits."

Write down *who* your customer is. Don't worry about age, sex, or social class. **Who** are they? What's **important** to them? What do they **value**? This isn't an easy task, so take your time with it:

_____

_____

_____

_____

_____

_____

_____

_____

_____

_____

_____

_____

CHAPTER 4

AGAINST WHOM?

In old-fashioned, Western movies it seemed there was only one of everything. Before the duel, the camera would scan the dusty street past signs that said, "Baker," "Cobbler," "Saloon," or "Bank." That was it. If the town already had one, you had to go be something else. A haberdasher perhaps.

"Who's your competition?"

"I don't really have competition. The other accounting firms are the big national places that do the books for huge offices."

Nashua, New Hampshire, is a modest town, but it's not quite like the Old West. Stacy has competition in places she hasn't thought of yet.

"No, seriously," she said. "I like working with small businesses of like 2 to 10 people."

"And nobody else does that?"

"Not that I've heard of, no."

Stacy makes a good living by organizing the finances of a couple auto repair shops, a boutique clothing store, a diner, and a nice jewelry store. But she just brought on part-time help, and she needs to keep him busy.

"I'd betcha there's 3 or 4 businesses right here that need me," she said, pointing to Canal Street on a map on her laptop.

"How are they doing their books now?"

"They do it themselves, or use Quicken, or wait until the end of the year and drop all their stuff off at that H&R Block across the street."

Stacy just rattled off four competitors:

1. Do it themselves

2. Quicken, or some other software

3. Not doing it at all (time)

4. H&R Block

If there's four, you can be sure there's eight.

Competition has a way of hiding right in front of you, and it's not limited to just the businesses that are doing what you're doing. "I don't have time" is competing for your business. "Eh...my wife is good with numbers" is also your competition. Anyone or anything that can siphon business from you is now your competition, and you need to know who or what they are.

Refer back to chapter one and add the *other* competition you have and the position they have in the marketplace.

CHAPTER 5

UNIQUE IS A VERB

Mid-century ad giant Rosser Reeves coined a phrase that gets volleyed around quite a bit: **Unique Selling Proposition.** Its ubiquity is also its downfall. When asked to identify it, many businesses point to something like "great service," or "we'll match any price." Reeves wanted a **USP** to be a specific benefit to amplify in advertising copy. It needed to be something different, special, and *meaningful* to the consumer. It also needed to be something the competition could not, or would not, offer. That's the part that often gets missed: What are you able to do that your competition cannot or will not do?

Sometimes getting these things started requires taking it in little bites. The unique proposition:

Martinelli's Pizzeria is the finest pizza you'll ever taste. If you don't like it, Michael Martinelli will give you your money back and give you $20 to buy a new pizza from anyplace you want.

"Are you kidding? Absolutely not. That doesn't even make sense. People are assholes. They'll screw me every day. What's gonna keep people from just telling me they hate the pizza and taking the 20 bucks?"

"Nothing. That *could* happen. But didn't you tell me you give people their money back if they come in and complain about the pizza?"

"Of course. That's the right thing to do," Michael said.

"And didn't you give that one couple a gift card to your competition?"

Do the math. Martinelli's averages about 400 pizzas each day. More on the weekends, and not so much on Tuesday. One month at Martinelli's equals close to 10,000 beautiful pizzas.

"When was the last time somebody complained?"

Straining to remember, Michael finally said, "August."

"August? Like, eight months ago August?"

"Yeah. I got good pizzas."

"So, these complaints don't happen all that often."

"No. Maybe a few times a year. I got good pizzas!"

Let's assume Michael has no clue how many complaints he gets. Let's bump it up to 20 complaints a month. At that rate, he's paying out just under $5,000 at the end of the year (which is coming out of his *marketing* budget). The marketing *benefit*, however, is worth five times that amount. It's a promise so bold, you *have* to see what's so special about these pizzas.

But we still haven't solved Martinelli's "I'm gonna get screwed" problem. There will always be jackasses. But how many?

"Michael, if you heard this offer from another business, would you abuse it?"

"Of course not."

"Would any of your family or friends screw over that business?"

"Not if they want to stay my friends, they wouldn't."

As it turns out, most people are decent people. In fact, an overwhelming majority of the population are honorable and honest. Plan for the jackasses and anticipate that they will come. But don't let them deter you from such an amazing offer. The benefit far outweighs the losses.

"Ya know what I did?" Michael said, eight months into the campaign. "I set it up so that the people that wanted that refund had to tell me what went wrong. I learned some important stuff we could improve and made the assholes uncomfortable enough that they didn't pull the stunt twice."

Boom. Well done, Michael. By the end of the year, the average number of complaints about his pizzas stayed at a very manageable 1 or 2 per month. 400 pizzas per day increased to an average of 475 per day. An increase of 18.75%.

Other businesses have employed other bold claims:

- A plumber who promises to be on time, or you don't pay

- A jeweler who promises to replace a diamond if it is ever chipped or lost

- A car dealer willing to exchange your used car after 30 days if you don't love it

- A mechanic who guarantees your car won't break down after a tune up, or he fixes what went wrong for free

What are you already doing that you know your competition can't do, or won't do? Can you amplify it into a bold claim or promise, with few (or no) loopholes?

 **Unique Selling Proposition -** A phrase coined by Rosser Reeves in his book *Reality in Advertising.* The man who taught us that "M&Ms melt in your mouth, not in your hands," believed an advertisement should showcase what is unique about a product or service. But it doesn't stop there. Reeves had 3 rules for a USP:

1. "Each advertisement must make a proposition to the consumer. Not just words, not just product puffery, not just show-window advertising. Each advertisement must say to each reader: "Buy this product, and you will get this specific benefit."

2. "The proposition must be one that the competition either cannot, or does not, offer. It must be unique—either a uniqueness of the brand or a claim not otherwise made in that particular field of advertising."

3. "The proposition must be so strong that it can move the mass millions, i.e., pull over new customers to your product."

Don't let that last one freak you out. Reeves, of course, was trying to sell Colgate toothpaste and Bic pens. Your mileage may vary.

SIDEBAR TRIVIA: Rosser Reeves (among others) is often believed to be the basis for the character Don Draper in the AMC-TV series *Mad Men.*

PART TWO
LOOK INSIDE

CHAPTER 6

WHAT ARE YOU REALLY SELLING?

Jennifer Himura, VP of Mortgage Lending at Bristol Community Bank, scrunched her brows, hoping to coax an answer out of her head.

"Nothing," she finally said. "All the banks have a mortgage department. We all have to fill out the same forms, and if the wind is blowing right, we might have a better interest rate. Besides that, nothing. There's nothing different about us."

"What are you selling, Jennifer?"

"What am I selling? I'm selling mortgages. No different from what any other bank is doing."

"What are you *really* selling?"

That question is always a killer, but its purpose is to get us closer to a customer's motivation. We already know what "thing" the customer is coming to buy. That requires no special effort. But what are they employing this product or service to actually do?

This can be answered by playing the toddler game of "why?"

Customer wants a mortgage > **Why?** > To get money > **Why?** > To buy a house > **Why?** > To have a place to live > **Why?** > For protection > **Why?** > To care for her family > **Why?** > She loves her family and wants a nice home where they can grow.

"Jennifer, what are people *really* buying from you?"

"They're buying what a home can provide for their family."

"Isn't *that* interesting?"

Drill beneath the surface of what you're selling to learn what customers are *really* buying from you. The closer you get to that answer, the closer you'll get to that which motivates your customer.

Harvard's Clayton Christensen takes it even further by asking the question "what *job* did you *hire* this product to do?" Christensen's "jobs-to-be-done" theory forces you to look at things as the customer does. The attributes of the product or service will come later, first we have to figure out why the customer hired your product.

You "hire" an engagement ring to dazzle your fiancé and express your love. You "hire" a jet-ski to scream like a maniac while adrenaline pumps through your system. You "hire" designer clothes to make you feel attractive or project a certain image to others.

These examples are still a bit thin. While you might be able to make a reasonable "guess," the juicy stuff comes from observing and asking your customers.

What are you selling?

What are you *really* selling?

If this is tough to answer (and it often is), use the *toddler method* on the next page.

My customers are buying:

Why?

Why?

Why?

Keep why-ing until you can't take it anymore. Then do 3 more. Don't let your answers have anything to do with your company. Example: **Why?** *"Because we've been in business for 23 years and are family owned"* is not the answer you are looking for. This must be 100% through the customer's eyes.

"The customer rarely buys what the business thinks it sells him."

– Peter Drucker

CHAPTER 7

THE SHORTEST CHAPTER

"I know exactly what my customers want."

No you don't.

CHAPTER 8

WHAT THE CUSTOMER WANTS

Once you've opened your business, or become responsible for marketing for your employer, you are hopelessly biased. You are on the other side of the looking glass, Alice. Regardless of how hard you squint, meditate, or trust your gut, you're still guessing.

Rajan "Roger" Singh, a fastidious accountant, pulled up a spreadsheet that was *not* populated with debits and credits. Instead, it was a wonderful collection of data he was able to capture from his customers. Like Charlie Lenz in Chapter 3, Roger has a good handle of "what" his customers are. Age, sex, income, tax brackets, net worth, zip codes, and so forth. He also had a handle on *who* his customers are.

"Married, white collar, and very busy," Roger said.

Depending on your personality, you might be a poet, or you might be a "quant." Quantitative types like things in order, logical, and mathematical. Poets, or qualitative types, are looking for things that might appear fuzzier. "Very busy" is qualitative. It doesn't fit in a nice box, but it's as important as "makes more than $74,000 per year."

"I don't get this stuff," Roger said, "which is exactly why I did the survey."

Roger has impressive instincts. He recognizes that his wheelhouse is hard numbers, and not in the "mushy-messy-stuff," as he calls it.

The civil war between "Poets" and "Quants" is as predictable as cats and...things that aren't cats. The Poets, the *qualitative* people, resent the Quants because their information is presented as firm, undebatable, and professional. The Quant-people can't stand the Poets because they seem to get all the attention with their fancy cursive writing and elegant prose. But Roger gets it.

"It's like this: The data is like the foundation and frame of the house. The angles have to be at 90 degrees, and the load-bearing walls have to be in place. But that mushy stuff (poetry), is like the style. Colonial, Art Deco, Tudor, whatever. You can't have one without the other."

To achieve good poetic data, you ask open-ended questions. You are looking for more than one-word answers.

- What do you like most about doing business here?

- What would you change, if you could?

- Before you did business here, did you have any hesitations or questions?

- What have you told friends about this business?

- What were you less than satisfied with?

- Anything else you would like us to know?

They can be any question you want, as long as it helps you gain some new knowledge or discover some limitations. Roger, ever the accountant, makes an important observation:

"There's no math here. You can't scale this fuzzy stuff."

Exactly. These are human insights. Personality quirks. Observations from the outside you will never see and your friends won't tell you.

"Busy. That's what I kept seeing over and over again. Busy. I got the math and logic just fine. I missed the 'why'."

Understanding that his customers were turning to him because they are "busy" becomes an important element in Singh's ad campaign. Without this poetic information, he may have spent time talking to people about his certifications, services, and size of his company. Instead, Roger has found insight into what he's *really* selling.

What questions would you ask your customers? Use some of the examples given and customize them for your business.

Quantitative Data – Information that can be measured with numbers. This information can be *quantified* and you can apply mathematical equations to it.

Qualitative Data – Information that does not have numerical data. "I like my job," "my kids are very busy," or "The Rolling Stones are better than Coldplay," are examples of qualitative information. You cannot apply math to qualities.

CHAPTER 9

WHICH CHILD IS YOUR FAVORITE?

"It's all important!"

He wasn't mad. Dr. Jeb Mason is just really intense. As a dentist, he already didn't like the idea of advertising. None of his peers advertise, so there was some pride that needed to be packed away. That wasn't what got him barking, however.

"Listen, I'm a general dentist. I do everything from cleanings to crowns. I take care of kids, and I can make your grandmother's dentures. Don't tell me it's not all important."

"I didn't tell you that."

"You said to pick one thing. I can't pick one thing. I can't make any money if I pick one thing."

"I didn't tell you to stop doing the other things. I asked which *one* do you want to be known for?"

"Didn't you hear me? People need to know I do it all. It's a one-stop shop."

Focusing your message is a hard thing to do. For the feisty business owner, it's *Sophie's Choice*. "Don't make me choose!" she implores. "Can't we just put just one more thing in there? Maybe just a mention?" (Apologies to William Styron...and Meryl Streep).

"To focus" inherently means to "sacrifice" something else. When a photographer focuses on a cow, he cannot *also focus* on the trees. A woman in labor is encouraged find a focus point, so she isn't *also focused* on the pain, the baby, and the fact that a room full of strangers are all looking up her gown. Focus your money on a good investment, and you get big returns. Focus on your diet, and you lose weight. Focus works.

This doesn't mean you stop doing the other things. It just means you **choose** what to market and what to sacrifice.

"Dr. Mason, have you ever been to Red Lobster?"

"Yes."

"Did you get seafood?"

"What kind of a question is that?"

Red Lobster's menu is well populated with *non*-seafood options. Chicken linguine, potato bacon soup, and a Caesar salad can all be had at Red Lobster. But a place called "Red Lobster" would be foolish to market that stuff. It's for the "...seafood lover in you," after all.

FedEx only tells us about their overnight delivery. They also deliver 2 day, medical specimens, and international freight on a big ship. But they shut up about it.

"Could you imagine Red Lobster doing ads for meatloaf?"

"Probably not," Dr. Mason said, starting to grasp the concept.

After some (welcome) quiet reflection, it all starts to make sense to him. The most profitable thing he does each day are kid's teeth cleanings.

"Do you like doing that, Doctor?"

"Absolutely. Kids love coming here. It's not terribly labor heavy, and if they have a good experience, the parents start making appointments for themselves."

Dr. Mason revamped his advertising to become the dentist kids love. This didn't require much adjustment internally. He was already doing it, already making money at it, and he enjoys kids.

Sophie's choice wasn't so tough after all. Taking a page from McDonald's, Dr. Mason made the whole thing an adventure for kids. Complete with a surprise reward at the end.

"I have these Moms sitting in the waiting area, and they're looking at brochures for teeth whitening. About every fourth kid that comes in, the Mom makes an appointment for teeth whitening."

"A rising tide lifts all boats" proved itself true for Dr. Mason. If he tried to "also focus on" all the other things he does, he loses his identity. He stops being unique. Everything gets blurry, and he fades into the background never to be noticed by the customer.

What is the most profitable thing you do?

Does it happen to match up with an available hole in the market?

Can you claim that as a position?

Can you live with the idea of being known for that and that only?

CHAPTER 10

THE SMALL END OF THE WEDGE

Find something in your business that requires the least amount of friction to get a customer started with you. Start with the small end of the wedge and use that to push the door open. For a bank, this might be a checking account, which leads to a savings account, which leads to a car loan, which leads to a mortgage. For Dr. Mason, cleaning a kid's teeth got him to Mom, and she wanted teeth whitening. A jeweler might choose to begin with the engagement ring, knowing that the engagement ring leads to wedding bands, which leads to Valentine's day gifts, which leads to anniversary jewelry. But the small end of the wedge is the engagement ring.

"Oil changes? I don't make crap on oil changes."

Marquis Auto Repair had been in the family for three generations. A good transmission replacement was a great day at work for Keith and his sons.

"I need more brake jobs and transmission replacements. Hell, we're good at fixin' transmissions too. Why can't we be the transmission fixin' place?"

There's nothing wrong with that strategy, and as discussed in the previous chapter, being known for one thing is always better than being known for too many things (or nothing at all).

"What do you do in these oil changes?"

"Everything. This isn't Walmart. New filter, lube the chassis, and everyone takes a part of the car. John looks at the brakes, Lee is on the radiator fluid, and whoever is under the car is looking for transmission leaks and is at the muffler. We don't miss much."

The Marquis family just found their wedge. Oil changes aren't all that profitable. But it's a way in. If he can get more oil changes, he has more opportunities to see cars. Out of 10 cars that come in, 3 of them will need something else.

"I'm not a snake about it. People have been coming here since grandpa. I tell the boys, 'if they don't need it, do

NOT sell it.' But at the same time, don't let anyone drive out of here if the car isn't safe."

Keith is playing the long game here. While he isn't making a fortune changing oil, people in town know they can get one done without an appointment, and he and his sons are super quick. They've built up a lot of goodwill, and nobody questions him when he says they need a new set of brakes. The oil change is just a handshake that introduces people to the rest of the shop.

Do you have a wedge?

How can you maximize it?

CHAPTER 11
ADVERTISING VS. MARKETING

Marketing is not advertising. But advertising is part of marketing.

Before we get too deep into building a campaign, it's important to acknowledge the difference between *marketing* and *advertising.* The two words are often used as synonyms, but advertising is merely one ingredient in marketing.

Marketing is the whole megillah. Marketing questions whether your price is right. Marketing wants to know about your suppliers and front-line staff. Marketing checks your product or service for flaws and benefits. Marketing needs to know that your business is easy to do business with, that it has a good location, an intuitive website, or wide availability of your product. Marketing also comes into play in the promotion of your product or service. It might include the skills of your sales staff, public relations, and advertising.

You can go nuts listing out all the things that marketing touches upon. You're probably better off assuming that if it's a part of your business that touches the customer, it's a part of marketing. Your receptionist and bathrooms; your pricing and nice business cards; training your sales staff and sweeping your foyer; and of course, your advertising.

Building a marketing plan involves:

Diagnosis: What the heck is going on? What's happening in the marketplace? What attributes do you have going for you? What qualitative, quantitative, and secondary data can you assemble?

Strategy: To build a strategy, you have to answer 3 questions:

Who: When you ask "who," you are trying to understand them as humans. Outdated "demographics" will not give you this answer. What do these people value? Why do they make the decisions they do? What do they have in common? What don't they have in common with those not in this segment?

I'm serious about the "demographics" thing. Stop saying it, stop using it, stop leaning on it. It's thin information that will get you nowhere. It's an amateur's crutch used by sloppy marketing people. Go deeper. You can do it. Correction: You must.

What: What are your objectives? (If you just said "to sell people stuff," you're probably still peddling demographics.) There could be any number of things that need to happen in a marketing strategy. Are you changing perceptions? Are you bolstering one product line over another (the wedge)? Are you addressing something internal? Is this a quick promotion? Is it long term brand building?

How: How will you position your company in their minds? This is going to take some studying of your competition. First, who is your competition? The local firms doing the same thing you are? The national firms doing the same things you are? The alternative of *not* doing business with you? Now that you've identified your competition... what position do they hold? Luxury? Fast-n-Cheap? Heritage? New and innovative? You can slice it 78 different ways, but don't get paralyzed by it. What's missing? What's open? When you've identified it, how do you plan to dramatize your place in the mind of the consumer?

Tactics: Sometimes called the "4 Ps of Marketing." This covers your pricing, distribution channel (the path from vendor to customer), your product, and the promotion of the product (which *includes* advertising).

This means that advertising is just 1/4 of 1/3rd of the whole megillah (I'm trying to bring that word back). That doesn't mean advertising is insignificant. All of these elements are equally important. If you screw up one, the others are neutered.

This is the order. There is no other order it can go in:

The strategy *must* come before tactics. The strategy *must* dictate the tactics. If somebody tells you *where* to advertise before doing the diagnosis and strategy, that person is stealing your money. I beg that you remember that:

If somebody gives you tactics <u>before</u> strategy, you are being robbed.

Advertising is the exciting, sexy, and creative face you put forward. It's what everyone sees, and so it gets a disproportionate amount of attention. But *don't think about* **where** you advertise until you have a strategy.

Every seller of every media will disagree, but:

"Never ask a barber if you need a haircut."

– Warren Buffett

CHAPTER 12

THE QUESTIONS

The following are useful questions to ask before building an advertising campaign:

How will you measure success? What exactly are you trying to do here? How will you know when you've arrived? Be specific and don't do anything else until this is answered.

How/why did you get into this business? Is there a compelling story that resonates beyond "to make money" that could be relevant? Is this your vocation? Your passion?

What are you offering the customer? And how is it different from your competitors?

Who is the competition? As we learned earlier, your competition isn't just businesses like yours that do the same thing. You are competing against time, DIY solutions, and everything on the internet.

Are there misconceptions about your product/service that you need to overcome? Is there a perception out there about your business category, i.e. "All used-car salesmen are crooks." While not accurate, these perceptions do exist in people's minds.

Are there misconceptions about your company? Are people not doing business with you because they don't know about you?...or because they *do* know about you and what they know isn't good?

What position are you trying to claim? This takes some in-depth work. As we saw in the first chapter, you need to know where everyone else sits and discover what is available to you. To really get into this, I'd suggest picking up a copy of *Positioning: The Battle for Your Mind* by Jack Trout and Al Ries. It is the seminal guide on the subject and is required reading in top marketing classes.

What triggering event happens just before the customer wants/needs your product or service? We're trying to find out what's going on in the customers' lives that will make them need you.

Do I need your product/service...or do I want it? I *need* water and food. I *want* a cleaning service. I *need* a furnace to make it through winter. I *want* a custom-built closet system. I *need* to get my taxes done. I *want* a really cool smartwatch.

Fill out the (good ol', tried-and-true) SWOT analysis, which seeks to uncover your:

Strengths

Weaknesses

Opportunities

Threats

What are you most proud of?

What will you always do, no matter what? In other words, what do you do that will never change in your business? What do you believe so strongly that it's a core value of what your business stands for, and nothing will ever change it?

What prevents people from doing business with you? Are there any points of friction that might slow a potential customer down, i.e. I can't pay for the engagement ring all at once, I have to be a member of your credit union, or I need a permit from the city before adding onto my house.

Do you have any guarantees? What is the "or else" clause in your guarantee? If "X" doesn't happen, you'll get "Y" in return. "If I can't get your roof done in one day, I'll write you a check for $1000." It has to be something so strong it cannot be ignored.

What do you want people who didn't do business with you today to know? You need to leave behind a thought, concept, or promise to those who do not yet need your product or service.

When someone chooses you over a competitor, do you know why?

When someone chooses your competitor over you, do you know why?

When someone at a cocktail party asks you what you do for a living, what do you say?

These are not the only questions worth asking. Each question you ask yourself (or have somebody ask you), must get you closer to that magical thing that makes your business special. Even the owner of the most predictable sports bar (28 TVs, pennants, hockey sticks and baseball bats screwed into the wall, and some kind of fried onion thing on the menu), got into business because he saw a hole in the marketplace. Something was missing, and this guy knew in his heart-of-hearts he was able to fill that need.

You are digging down to the nuclear core of your business' story. It's the acorn from which everything grows. It's the keystone that holds it all together. The spark that made you get up one morning, put your family's future on the line, and open a business. It's time to find that again.

It doesn't matter whether your answers are or aren't used in the advertising. The purpose of this exercise is to find stories. Electric stories. A passion that must be admired.

PART THREE
PULLING IT TOGETHER

CHAPTER 13
HOW TO BUILD A CATHEDRAL

Advertisements stand alone. Campaigns are a string of advertisements with a golden thread between them.

A brick is a rectangular block of clay and shale. A Cathedral is the assemblage of many bricks in a predefined pattern.

Business owners often try to get the whole cathedral in one advertisement. These are the numbing ads that list every single thing a company does, *and* their hours, *and* their phone number, *and* their Thursday specials, *and* how many square feet are in the place, *and* the year they went into business, *and and and and...*

How do you build a cathedral? One brick at a time. As the architect of your ad campaign, you start with your blueprint. This is your strategy (refer back to chapter 11).

Once you've designed your strategy, you get to make it pretty. Each brick you add in this string of advertisements must support the strategy. If the strategy of your campaign is to build a cathedral, each ad must hold the cathedral up.

An easy case study is Geico. Each ad in the campaign is designed to support one strategy. "Give us 15 minutes, and we'll save you 15% on car insurance." Did you know Geico also sells insurance for your pet?...for your jewelry?...for your business? No, you don't. Because that's not the strategy. The strategy is to sell car insurance. If they started throwing all that other stuff in, they would just have an unrecognizable pile of bricks. Put simply: If you try to be known for everything, you end up being known for nothing.

If your goal is to be known as the accountant who saves companies money, you need to assemble the ads in a way that supports that one idea. One ad could be about organizing taxes...to save a company money. The next ad could be about simplifying the billing process...to save a company money. A third ad could be about aggressive budgeting...to save a company money. All ads end up in the same place. They might be 3 different ads, but they all point to the same nucleus.

A cathedral cannot be built in a day. It will take many bricks, a long time, and a good plan. But you can do it...one brick at a time.

CHAPTER 14

HABITUATION

What do a choo-choo train, paint thinner, alcohol, and boring ads all have in common? Once they become common, they will kill you.

Habituation fascinates me. In psychology, when you are exposed to the same thing repeatedly, the thing eventually becomes so common that you are no longer aware of it. Ever know someone who lives near the train tracks?

"How can you stand that?"

"Eh...eventually you don't hear it anymore."

This is why otherwise sensible people in metropolitan areas walk right in front of a speeding passenger train.

When you work with paint thinner, you're warned to get out of the room every 30 minutes for fresh air. After continued exposure to that smell, it becomes so common that you forget you're being slowly poisoned.

This nasty quirk of our brain is there to protect us. If you constantly felt the clothes against your skin, or actively listened to every whir of the air conditioner, you'd go nuts. The brain tucks these things away, saying, "I got that info...I don't need it over and over again."

The same is true with advertising. If I show you 10 ads for cars, it's highly likely that many of them will feature the car going impossibly fast across the Bonneville Salt Flats. If not there, they will show the car making smooth turns on a tight road upon a mountain in Northern California.

Advertising is full of these tropes, and you owe it to the life of your company to learn them.

Retirement plans: Show an active elderly couple on the beach.

Prescription drugs: Mandatory doctor in a lab coat holding a clipboard.

Restaurants: Must have close up shot of a head of lettuce being chopped in half as water droplets burst from the leaves in slow motion. This will be followed by sliced tomatoes falling from an unknown height and landing perfectly on an open sandwich.

Coffee: Show a weathered, old worker happily filling a burlap sack of beans in his far away country. Cut to a suburban woman in a robe waving to her children, as she inhales the "rich aroma" of her warm drink.

This could go on for pages. The local car dealer with an obnoxiously bright print ad packed with pretty cars and prices in double-bold type. The overused scenario of a silly husband who just doesn't get it, but *Mom* will come in and save the day.

Yes. We've all seen that movie. We already know how it ends.

This sameness in advertising is its downfall. By themselves, these look like perfectly lovely, and accurate, ads. But when you stack them side-by-side, they start to get blurry. After they get blurry, they fade into the background thanks to habituation.

To break through, something (anything!) different has to happen. You only notice the whir of your air conditioner when something goes KLANG! You are completely unaware of the feeling of the shirt against your skin, until that jerk of a tag starts scratching your neck. You want your commercial to stand out on a rock radio station? Try putting a banjo in the background.

Your approach has to be different than everything around it. It must be different. The message still needs to be useful and meaningful to the customer, but you absolutely must approach it from an unexpected angle.

If Bounty paper towels told you that they "absorb spills fast," you'd shrug your shoulders and move on. Bounty, however, is "The Quicker-Picker-Upper."

Spend your time and money right here. Make that message have an approach that's never been tried. Make yourself, and your industry, a little uncomfortable. Be the tag in the shirt that gets people's attention.

CHAPTER 15
A GOLDEN THREAD

"I found my tonic note," said Sue-Ann, the home-cleaning pro we met earlier.

"Tonic note?"

"I sing in the choir at Third Pres. Our conductor was talking about 'tonic notes.' That's the note at the beginning of the song and the resolve of a song. It's kinda like 'home base.' It's the note that holds the whole song together."

"And your tonic note is...?"

"Flat-Rate Cleaning."

Sue-Ann found her "Golden Thread." It's the part of an ad campaign that sews it all together. To create a *campaign* requires creating a series of ads that all come back to a

73

single point.

Capital One credit cards will present you with scenarios ranging from Vikings to Samuel L. Jackson...but their **Golden Thread** challenges you to consider all the rewards Capital One offers, versus the rewards your card *doesn't*. It's all punctuated with: "What's in Your Wallet?" Nike sells you shoes, shirts, and golf balls with the decree "Just Do It." Nike's slogan first appeared in 1988, and has not wavered. If you want to start your day like an Olympian, you must choose "Wheaties: The Breakfast of Champions." A declaration they've made since 1935. Motel 6 tells the weary traveler many things about the roadside motel. But no matter which attribute is in the spotlight of the commercial, Tom Bodett will promise that if you need an inexpensive place to stay, they will always "leave the light on for ya." A Golden Thread that has survived over 3 decades. Wise companies from Maxwell House Coffee (Good to the Last Drop) to M&M's (Melts in Your Mouth, Not in Your Hands) to Engergizer Batteries (It Keeps Going and Going and Going) all understand that fierce consistency and a reliable Golden Thread is what holds their brand image together. The temptation to "try something fresh" can be overwhelming. But wise Chief Marketing Officers in those companies know the risk of changing is just too great.

Once Sue-Ann had found that Golden Thread or her "tonic note," making her whole campaign became easy. There was no question about where each ad was going, the only thing left to figure out was *how* to get to that destination.

Once Sue-Ann decided that, without exception, she was going to quote a flat-rate to every customer who called, the campaign's job became to *prove* to new customers she would do just that.

It began with a post card. For Sue-Ann, this made sense because she only wanted to clean houses in her immediate area. She also wanted to be sure that this idea would work, so testing it on a small scale gave her some important data.

The postcard was a vintage photo of a messy living room. No logo and no writing on the front. To the recipient, this looked like somebody just sent them a postcard. On the back was a written note from Sue-Ann:

"I guess those magic elves didn't show up last night. Again. I don't know much magic, but I do know I can whip any 3 rooms like that into spick-span shape for just $149. You pick the 3 rooms, we'll be your magic elves. Don't care how big. Don't care how long it takes. You point to 3 rooms in your place, and for $149 there's no part that doesn't get clean."

The next postcard, again designed to look like an actual postcard and not an ad, had this note:

- ☐ *My Bedroom*

- ☐ *Kids Bedroom*

- ☐ *Guest Bedroom*

- ☐ *Living Room*

- ☐ *Kitchen*

- ☐ *Dining Room*

- ☐ *Office*

Pick 3 for $149 flat. No part doesn't get clean. Guaranteed.

A few weeks later, a follow-up postcard went out that said:

"No kidding. Pick the 3 biggest rooms in your house. I don't care which ones. They'll get cleaned for $149 flat. No part of those rooms doesn't get clean. No kidding."

The pattern should be clear. The campaign has a singular focal point. It can be approached from an infinite number of directions, but it always has to find its way back to the "flat rate."

The skeptic says: "'No part doesn't get clean?' That's a weird way to say that."

YES! It is. You are up against a serious glut of things that look, sound, and feel exactly the same. Habituation is a sonuvabitch. It's not about to let you through its fenced-up border unless you shake things up a bit.

Anything Sue-Ann does from this point on, she will always end up in the same place – the $149 flat rate. Her truck is wrapped with a big $149 on the side. She leaves behind a refrigerator magnet die-cut in the shape of $149. When Sue-Ann's receptionist answers the phone, she says, "Sue-Ann's Spick and Span. Which three rooms can we clean for $149?"

There are some serious limitations here. Sue-Ann is going to have to address what happens in a few years when she inevitably increases her rates. Also, if she is to expand to other neighborhoods, $149 may be a money loser for her.

"I've got a secret," she says. "The $149 thing? That just gets me in the door. Right now, only 'bout 30% of my customers do that. Once they try it out, it's damned easy to sell 'em on a regular contract."

Sue-Ann found a wedge, and it's working.

CHAPTER **16**

A BOLD PROMISE

AARON BURR: *Good luck with that, you're takin' a stand. You spit. I'm a'sit. We'll see where we land.*

JOHN LAURENS: *Burr, the revolution's imminent. What do you stall for?*

ALEXANDER HAMILTON: *If you stand for nothing, Burr, what'll you fall for?*

Seven minutes into Lin-Manuel Miranda's masterpiece *Hamilton*, the forgotten founding father lands a philosophical blow to the man who would eventually cut him down.

I hear this question two ways:

1: If you have no commitment to a cause, why even

bother?

2: If you have no firm beliefs, how easily are you duped?

Miranda asks a worthwhile question. What *do* you stand for? If I ask 50 people about you or your business, can they clearly answer that? Clearly. Not a fuzzy kinda-sorta...but an *emphatically clear answer.*

Brace yourself, because standing **for** something also means standing **against** something. Some people just aren't gonna dig your business. What do you stand against? What customers do you not want?

It seems counter intuitive to suggest there are customers you don't want...because, ya know, money. But, it is indeed an important question to ask.

Herb Kelleher, founder of Southwest Airlines, set out to build a discount airline. At the time, flying was only for those who had the means. Kelleher's mission was to invent THE low-fare airline. This meant that anything that may cause Southwest to raise their prices unnecessarily needed to be eliminated. No meals. No first class. A purely functional airline that got everyday people from place to place. Kelleher tells of a time when his wealthy friends said they would love to fly his new airline, but they **only** fly first class. "Put a few rows of first class seats in your planes Herb, and I'll gladly fly Southwest." Herb said, "No thank you, you'll have to find another airline."

An undeniable <u>commitment</u> to a belief. He had a pack of wealthy business executives willing and ready to hand over MORE money than he would usually make, but Herb said, "No thank you."

Kelleher knows who his customers are, and *who they are not.* Southwest continues to be the lone airline that has posted a profit for 43 straight years. That includes the recessions in 1981, 1990, 2001, and 2007. He has outlasted giants like Pan Am, Eastern, TWA, Northwest, and Branniff.

You can't tell me what any of those last 5 airlines stood for. Or against. You do know, with undeniable clarity, what Southwest stands for. And against.

ALEXANDER HAMILTON: *Why should a tiny island across the sea regulate the price of tea?*

AARON BURR: Alexander, please!

ALEXANDER HAMILTON: Burr, I'd rather be divisive than indecisive, drop the niceties.

If you stand for nothing, what is it all for?

CHAPTER 17
KILLER CLICHES

I wrote my first ad when Ronald Reagan was still President of the United States. A fellow writer leaned over and said, "See that? That line? That's the biggest cliché in advertising. Don't ever use it."

The line was "For all your car care needs." I went back through other ads I had written. Jesus Christ! It's all over the place.

For all your home improvement needs.

For all your retirement planning needs.

For all your hardware needs.

For all your banking needs.

For all your garage door needs.

We are a needy people apparently. What is astonishing to me is that decades, and five presidents, later that line continues to be used and abused. A Google search for "All Your Car Care Needs" comes back with 91,600 businesses. "For All Your Home Improvement Needs" yields north of 394,000 businesses. Do you have "remodeling needs?" I have 2,183,492 places to help satisfy that need.

These ad-crutches abound in many forms:

- "Your one-stop-shop for..."

- "Conveniently located..."

- "Your _____ headquarters."

- "We have a friendly, knowledgeable staff."

- "The biggest selection, the finest quality, the greatest customer service." *Superlatives are horribly common. And just plain "horrible."*

- "We care about you, our customer."

- "But it's our people that make the difference."

- "You've tried the rest, now try the best."

- "Your satisfaction is guaranteed."

- "Fast and friendly service."

Unfortunately the word "cliché" doesn't adequately

describe these deadly phrases. If you look at them, you see that all you are promising is to be *about* as good as the customer expects you to be. *You're going to be friendly?* I kinda hope so. *You have a big selection?* Yeah, I expect you to have the crap I'm looking for. *Your staff is knowledgeable?* It's your company, I hope to holy-hell you know what you're talking about. *You guarantee my satisfaction?* Could you be a little more vague? *You're conveniently located?* How do you know where I am? That's kinda freaking me out.

All of these claims are not only devoid of specifics, they are the very least I expect of a company. You're sorta obligated to be polite if you want to stay in business. You kinda need to know what you're talking about. I pretty much expect you'll have what I'm looking for.

You get no points for doing what is expected of you. The trouble with these clichés is not just how common they are. The trouble is that you are using good advertising time to say absolutely nothing. If I can take your name out and seamlessly plug another business name in its place, you probably have a very common commercial.

Start again.

CHAPTER 18

NOWS OR LATERS?

People are in the market to buy what you're sellin' today. There are also people who are not shopping right now, but they will need you someday. Have you chosen which group to speak to?

The "Nows" are very attractive because they have money in their hands, and they are looking for someone to give it to. Now. You get their "now" money by telling them that if they don't come to you right now, they will miss out on a great opportunity, and there will never be another chance to ever give you money ever again. This is the JCPenney approach. There are only two days to save, and after that you will have to pay full price! *Until next weekend, when we do it all over again.*

The "Laters" are the ones who don't need you now. They may not even *know* they need you at all. The "Laters" are going about their day, taking care of their families, eating candy bars, and putting gas in the gas tank.

Good sense would suggest that you must go after the "Nows." But your good sense isn't all that good. When you advertise to the "Nows," you can get them, and there ain't nothing wrong with that. But you've also put an expiration date in their heads. "You must come before Sunday to get this thing. If you don't, you'll miss out." This leaves almost nothing in the minds of the "Laters." They have no reason to remember you, because you just told them to stop thinking about you Sunday.

The "Nows" are also a smaller population. On any given Saturday, let's pretend 3% of the city needs new mattresses. You and the other mattress stores are fighting over that little clump of people by holding the "biggest sale of the year." You might even get some of them.

But consider this: The rest of the city, 97%, will need a mattress **someday**. Everyone will need a mattress *someday*. If you consistently and deliberately tell the "Laters" why you're special and what you believe in, the day the "Laters" become the "Nows," you have first position in their minds.

If you're thinking about brands of mattresses right now, do the names Sealy and Serta come to mind? That's not a lucky guess. They are the biggest brands, and they advertise consistently (If you're thinking Tempur-Pedic, that's also Sealy. If you're thinking Simmons or Beauty Rest, that's Serta). If you thought Select Comfort, well done. That's #3 in the marketplace. Now for the crazy thing: Nobody reading this is thinking Corsicana Bedding or Comfort Solutions. Those are not fly-by-night companies, they're numbers 4 and 5 in mattresses.

Did you get all of that? If you're not in the top 3, you are virtually unknown.

Damn. If you're not being considered, you're not in the game.

Slow and steady wins the race. Aesop already taught you that. Marathon runners know it, and it seems successful brands know it too.

Think of a local HVAC place. Now think of a local dentist. Now think of a local car dealership. Now a plumber. I bet the most successful ones in town are the ones that came to mind.

...and I bet they all know the power of talking to the "Laters."

CHAPTER 19

C.F. HATHAWAY'S FORMULA

A tiny, men's shirt company in Waterville, Maine, was hidden by the shadow of giants. By the time they had hired Dave to help with advertising, post-war, ready-made factory shirts were dominating the racks of department stores. In short, the company was (quite literally) losing its shirt.

Dave, a talented copywriter, had already written elegant words to match the quality of the shirts. A distinguished model was hired for the print ad, and a top New York photographer was ready to take pictures. Before arriving at the photography studio, Dave stopped at a drugstore to pick up some eyepatches.

Handing them to the photographer, he said, "Just shoot a couple of these to humor me. Then I'll go away, and

91

you can do the serious job."

David Ogilvy's "The Man in the Hathaway Shirt" ushered in a new era of storytelling in advertising. The story, however, took place entirely in your imagination. Before you stood a distinguished gentleman being measured by a tailor. Who is this guy? What happened to his right eye? Is he an aristocrat? A war veteran?

Whatever trauma befell the man in his past, he stands unflinching and proud. He's successful. Determined. Debonair. You must lean into this ad and try to figure out the story. You have no choice. Your brain won't let you pass it by. You want to be this one-eyed-guy.

The first ad placed in The New Yorker had cost $3,100. Before the week was over, you couldn't find a Hathaway shirt anywhere in the five boroughs.

The formula? The less money you have, the more curious energy your ad needs. The more competition you have eating up mindshare, the more quirk you must employ.

This doesn't mean being outrageous or insane (I'm looking at you, car dealers), it means you better add a little more paprika. Make me tilt my head just slightly and say "huh...what's up with that?" Break the pattern with something that doesn't belong, but fits.

Sometimes, it's as simple as a 50 cent eyepatch.

CHAPTER 20

AND DON'T FORGET
THE PAPRIKA

Sometimes it's used to simply add color to food. I've heard that quaint European cafes will have it on the table in place of salt and pepper, though I've not seen that. Paprika has a special zing. A quirky something that stops you. "Oh," you say, "what's that...what did you put in the..."

Now, don't be a fool. Put in too much paprika and you wreck the whole thing. Leave it out, and your dish has all the appeal of American cheese.

When you are cooking up an ad for your company, don't forget the paprika. Or nutmeg, if that's how you swing. Be brave enough to add a dash of curiosity to the advertisement. Something that knocks 4/4 time into an odd Brubeckian 5/4. You owe it to your company to make the bubble in the level just a hair off.

But don't be a lunatic about it. Overdo the paprika, and you end up with those ads that people enjoy, but nobody knows what they're about. They may be "talked about," but they aren't bringing customers to your door.

"In advertising," Bill Bernbach said, "not to be different is virtually suicidal.

"But that's too risky," you say.

It's too risky to not, I say.

Don't forget the paprika.

CHAPTER 21

WHERE IS YOUR CRACK?

Philadelphia is home to an iconic symbol of The United States of America. The Liberty Bell sits in Independence Hall, cracked. It split on its very first ding. Each year, a million people go look at a busted bell.

Have you ever seen a picture of the back of it? Neither have I. You can walk around the entire thing. But everyone who takes its picture, takes it from its most unattractive side. I wonder if it would be as compelling to us if it were perfect?

Marilyn Monroe and Cindy Crawford have moles. Ryan

Gosling's eyes don't line up, and Tom Cruise has a crooked nose, and his teeth are off center.

Starting to pick up what's going on? Years ago, a mentor of mine told me, "Don't make those commercials too slick...people will slide right off."

Where is the flaw in your ad? I want a tiny nail poking out of that ad so it snags my sweater when I walk by. Make me remember you like a broken bell.

Your ad campaign needs a crack for two reasons:

It keeps people from "sliding off" because the ad is "too perfect."

It shows customers you are real. You are filled with flaws and foibles. So am I.

When Orson Wells put together his radio masterpiece "War of the Worlds," he wrote mistakes into the script. It made the listener believe it was live, because it was imperfect.

CARL PHILLIPS: *Ladies and gentlemen (Am I on?). Ladies and gentlemen, here I am, back of a stone wall that adjoins Mr. Wilmuth's garden...*

Think of architecture oddities that compel us: the John Hancock Center, the Leaning Tower of Pisa, the Burj Khalifa, and the St. Louis Arch.

They're not like the other kids.

A poor marketer would look at the Colosseum in Rome and whine, "ehh...it's all...can't we get some drywall and even it out...?"

A good marketer says: "You're beautiful just as you are."

People are craving authenticity more than ever before. If you want to show me that you are the real deal, show me your scars.

CHAPTER 22

TELL ME A STORY

"I was about 8 or 9, I think," John said, his eyes meandering over his desk. He has a voice that sweeps the room clean. Ignoring him isn't an option. His words handcuff you.

"I went to work one day with my Pop. You've never seen somebody work so hard and get nowhere." An upturned palm appeared from under the desk, and he jabbed it with his left index finger.

"Right there. His boss walked in and put 9 pennies...right...there. He took a tenth penny and put it here," patting his shirt pocket. "You know what that means?"

"No."

"Pay yourself. Always pay yourself first."

John's mouth puckered, and he drank in a big breath through nostrils that looked like the business end of a shotgun.

"So, Pop looks at me. Looks at my shirt pocket. Looks back at old man Smolak. I got it. I don't think Pop ever did."

"What makes you so sure, John?"

"Pop would have given his left leg for a business like this," he replied, thumping his sausage-like finger on his desk. "He just couldn't close the deal. Ya know why?"

"Why?"

"Never invested in himself. You gotta invest in yourself. Warren said that."

"Warren?"

"Buffett!"

John dropped more names than an amateur juggler. He didn't know Warren Buffett, but quotes would come rolling out like so many gumballs from a machine.

"I guess I'm sayin' that's why you're here. Pop never would have spent money on advertising. I dunno...maybe it was The Depression. He trusted his mattress, that's it. He wasn't a bad guy, quite the contrary. He just wasn't a business guy."

"An entrepreneur's life isn't for everyone"

"Mr. Smolak ended up giving me my first job. That guy was gut-smart, ya know what I mean? He just had a sense about business stuff. Not the egghead MBA stuff, but real things."

John Wells runs his company with clock-like precision. But there's a humanity in John I respect. He spends 93% of his time strengthening his staff.

"Happy employees equal happy customers. Easy to say. Hard to do. Ya can't get distracted by the petty shit," he said with a smile. "I believe in my employees. Every one of 'em. Smolak never fired anybody. Never. He helped them grow, and if they couldn't grow anymore, he helped them find their next career. Never seen anything like it."

Nothing you've read actually happened. It's a story. It's not a terribly good story. I wrote it in one sitting, while munching on a grilled chicken salad at Panera.

You've likely heard the saying "facts tell and stories sell." The brain loves a good story. Stories have been used to teach people since Unga Bunga first wrote on a cave wall. If you want people to remember, show them a story.

"Stories are more persuasive," according to Jonathan Gottschall, author of *The Storytelling Animal: How Stories*

Make Us Human. Gottschall studies how stories and art influence decisions in the brain. "Stories have really impressive cognitive power. In normal, waking-life, our minds are flitting all over the place. We have about 100 daydreams per hour. But when you're in a good story...you have approximately *zero* daydreams per hour. And, it's not just a state of high attention, it's a state of high *suggestibility.* People are more open-minded when they are inside story land. For better...and for worse."

Here are elements for good storytelling:

Don't tell, show. Instead of telling me that "George Washington was an honest politician," *show* me his honesty. The "*cherry tree murder*" was a fable. It never *tells* you "Washington was an honest dude." But it *shows* you his honesty through his behavior. Don't tell, show.

Be specific. Well written stories draw you in with specifics. John "thumped his desk with sausage-like fingers," is more interesting than just "pounding the desk." In ad-writing, instead of saying <u>"we have a wide variety of used cars,"</u> be specific and say <u>"we have 43 SUVs, 28 pickups, and 13 convertibles."</u> Plumbers shouldn't say they can "clear clogged drains." Instead, they should <u>"drag out the gloppy-gunk that has knotted up your pipes."</u> Regardless of which media you use for advertising, show me a vivid and specific picture using words.

Verbs > Adjectives. In the story, John didn't merely have a "very loud voice." You were told that his eyes "were *meandering* over his desk," and his voice "*sweeps* the room clean." "His words *handcuff* you." He didn't "take a big deep breath through his large nose," he "*drank* the air." Next time you read a compelling story or poem, notice the abundance of verbs and the lack of adjectives.

Stay in the present. As you tell me the story of your company, keep the action happening *right now*. For example, this is happening in the past: <u>"When you drove your kids to school this morning, did you hear squeaking coming from your brakes?"</u> This is happening now: <u>"As your car comes to a stop, children hide behind their parents, dogs faint, and cats bolt up trees. It's probably time for new brakes."</u>

Speak to me. Just me. Choose the pronoun "you." Assume that I'm the one you're trying to reach. Bad ads begin with: <u>"Attention accountants looking for work!"</u> Good ads know they are already speaking to the right person. <u>"You work numbers like a pastry chef. The puzzle of helping businesses keep the books in order and keeping more profits is what wakes you up every day. It's time you joined a company that is going to pay you for your talents."</u> Those who fit know who they are. Those who don't fit know somebody who does.

Start in the middle. Stories never (should) begin with "Once upon a time, there was a goat." Exposition is tedious. You don't need to "Brady Bunch" your story and drag out every tiny detail for me to figure out what's happening. A simple opening like "Mom! Where are my gym shoes!?", and I know we have a kid and a Mom, and everybody is running late. In John's story, we meet him in the middle of telling his own story. The puzzle pieces come together quickly. Next time you watch a movie or read a book, notice how the action is already going on before you got there.

You don't need to dine on great literature to be able to weave words into a solid advertisement. But you would do well to snack on some interesting poems and profound writings on a regular basis. You will start to notice some interesting ways to get your point across. Poetry is useful because its goal is to make you feel something very specific. Not into poetry? Dive into satire. Satirical comedy's job is to persuade you while making you laugh. Think about great works like *Catch 22*, *M*A*S*H**, or *All in the Family*. *Saturday Night Live* and *The Daily Show*. Even Rod Serling's *The Twilight Zone*. They have all brilliantly cloaked opinion with brilliant entertainment. Both poetry and satire are great ways to sneak past the logical brain and get on a superhighway to someone's heart.

CHAPTER 23

LOGIC IS THE MOST ILLOGICAL WAY TO ADVERTISE

"Just tell 'em the facts." Seems like a reasonable request. "I just want to educate the consumer." Aaaand that's where it breaks down. Nobody asked to be educated. Today is not the day people woke up craving a degree in dental health or knowledge about tire rotations. Tomorrow won't be either. So why, in our information craving society, is logic so illogical?

The answer is as old as the human race. Before the written word, the elders would pass stories down to the young. Stories are easy to remember. Facts are not. Cave writings were a sort of storyboard graffiti. Legends, myths, and fables were the tools of education. The Bible teaches through stories, and we know of George Washington's honesty by way of a conjured tale about a cherry tree.

After stories come emotions. The intuition of our ancestors to know the difference between safety and peril. The bond between mother and baby. Pride and fear. Shame and jubilation. Butterflies in the stomach. Not going on a date because of a "gut feeling."

The brainy people who study brains tell us that well over 90% of our decision making is made in the subconscious mind. Your brain already made a choice before "you" are conscious of it. You step up into your SUV because it makes you feel good. It also delivers a message about you. You say out loud that "I need an SUV because I go camping, and sometimes get lumber from the hardware store." But the auto industry tells us that well over 90% of SUV owners never once "sport" or "utility" in their "vehicle."

You buy your groceries from WalMart, Kroger, and Publix. Why not Aldi? Aldi is cheaper. Logic says we only care about price. But logic is a liar. It "makes sense" to eat at home for both health and financial reasons. How did restaurant revenue increase over $400 billion since 2000? Even with a couple of ugly recessions in there.

Our decisions are made emotionally. We might concoct a logical explanation for it, so we have something to say.

But emotions rule the roost. Why did (beautiful movie star) marry that dopey looking guy? Why do we judge the leader of the free world on likability? What did John Lennon see in Yoko Ono?

Why are you trying to apply logic to emotional things?

...and why are you trying to "educate" me through a commercial?

Tell me a good story.

CHAPTER 24

I'M AWESOME (NO YOU'RE NOT)

You're at a cocktail party, dreading the innocuous small talk. A toothy, over-tanned, hair-gelled gentleman catches your eye and it's over. Trapped in his tractor beam, you know he doesn't have an "elevator pitch," ...you're takin' the stairs.

"I'm the assistant manager at Hubert Telcom. I do interactive communication solutions. 'Telemarketing' for those not in the biz. Got up at 4:30 today. I'm doing the paleo thing. Off to Crossfit by 5. Signed on a new client today. Big name, can't reveal it now, but I crushed it in the presentation. I tell ya, work hard all day, but I play hard at night. Know what I mean?"

This is what bad advertising sounds like. A painful litany of what you do, how long you've been doing it, and vague claims of how excellent your service is. You believe that if you just read your company's resume out loud, the customer will have no choice but to do business with you.

Telling people "about your company" is (at best) a limp documentary. At worst, it comes off like the braggadocios blockhead at your cocktail party. Don't be that guy.

Your communication with your customer is more like a delicate courtship. Consider the classic rule of a first date: Don't talk about yourself, and be interested in the other person. If your ads don't talk to her about her, you're getting swatted away.

When crafting your ad, it needs to be at least 70% about the customer. You need to solve his problem or fill his need. It should happen in real time, present tense.

"You've never felt more relaxed as you sit under the sun and take in the ocean breeze," is much more interesting than "at Sandy Dune Resort we have 3 miles of beach and 5 star rated customer service for the past 18 years." The first one is about the customer. The second one is about as interesting as the paleo, Crossfit guy.

Don't expect the customer to connect the dots with

your boring biography. Take the story to the real reason they are seeking you for. I don't need your mortgage, I want a home for my family. Tell me I can have a home for my family, and I'll get your mortgage.

Most importantly, a courtship takes time. I need to trust, believe, and feel good about you. Too many ads try to jump right into bed, and that's no way to treat someone you want a relationship with.

CHAPTER 25

FIREWORKS AND SALES

In the U.S., fireworks always show up on July 4th. They sometimes show up on New Year's Eve. They occasionally appear after a home team home run. I think fireworks are pretty cool. If they're so nifty and always gather a crowd, why don't we have fireworks every day?

That should be an easy one to answer:

1. That would be astoundingly annoying

2. Fireworks would stop being special

3. Your dog would pack his bags and move to Peru

When you have a sale at your business, treat it like you're handling fireworks. Keep it rare and have a good reason to blow them off.

"But people love savin' money. Whenever I have a sale, it always gathers a crowd!"

If you are always having a sale, then you're never really having a sale (pay attention J.C. Penney, Kohl's, and every car dealer always). The reason to have a sale is to motivate people who are shopping for your product right now to consider you. The other reason is to nudge people who are maybe shopping to act today.

But am I really nudged to buy a refrigerator this week when it will certainly be on sale next week? You already answered this question when I asked you about fireworks. See rule #2. Do you think I'm dense enough to believe that "prices have never been lower," and "offer ends at midnight?" See rule #1.

Retailers should have sales. There's nothing wrong with a good ol' barnstormin' sale. But like fireworks, your sale will only work if you have a legitimate reason and it's rare.

Be very specific in your offer. "All men's sweaters are $30 this Saturday," is much clearer than "everything is 15% off all August."

Make sure there's really a reason for your sale. "Back to school" makes good sense for school supplies. "Back to school" isn't a reason to tune up your furnace.

Go big or just don't. I'm not going to the park to watch a kid play with sparklers. Your sale must be bold and *really* a sale.

Make it rare. Instead of offering a pretend $100 discount on a TV every month, why not stack it up and offer $600 off twice a year? That gets my attention, and it just might move me to action if I believe it's not going to happen again for another 6 months.

Sales come with risks (I'm told people like lists, so here's another one):

1. Sales cut into your profits.

2. Sales reduce your product to a commodity. If price is the only thing special about it, I may buy it from you today, then buy it from the place across the street tomorrow. Because, who cares?

3. Sales are only for the "now" customer. If I don't need a mattress now, your ad doesn't apply to me. You miss the opportunity to tell me why you're special so I remember you when I do need a mattress.

You're not enhancing your brand or solidifying your market position by having a sale. You're just having a sale. Professor Mark Ritson, a bit of a firecracker himself, offers this:

"Sales promotions are a notoriously stupid thing to do and [...] are something that should be resisted wherever possible. Yes, they shift a lot of stock and also help provide short-term differentiation for your brand over the competition. But that short-term sales bump comes with a much greater hangover as even the smallest cut in price causes financial disaster to bottom line profitability."

Ritson goes on to say that the only way to compensate for the loss of profit and brand identity "can only be resolved with...you guessed it...another sales promotion."

Slow and steady. Do it fast, and all you get are prefabricated homes in Levittown. Take your time, and you can build a cathedral.

CHAPTER 26

MAKING IT TO MILWAUKEE ON 10 GALLONS OF GAS

Your destination is Milwaukee. You have 10 gallons of fuel and 4 vehicles. You could put 2.5 gallons in each tank and "see what happens." Or, put all 10 gallons in one tank and have a chance at making it.

You already know the answer.

There are more than 4 advertising "vehicles" out there. It's tempting to want to test drive them all and "see what happens," but you rarely get to your destination. You haven't put enough gas in the tank to make any of them do

117

their job.

"But I don't want to miss talking to those people."

There will always be people you will not talk to. There's nothing you can do about it.

Advertising is a memory game. You want to be the name they remember. The only way to do that is to talk to the same people over and over and over again. There is no benefit to talking to a person once, then running over there to talk to another person, then running down the block to talk to a third. You end up "kind of" talking to 3 people and selling nothing. Find a group of people you can afford to talk to and tell them your story. A lot. You cannot predict when they will need you, so you'd better be in their head when that happens.

Who's driving? Words are driving. The difference between making an ad explode like a supernova or fizzle out like a match is your words. I don't care if it's on Facebook, a matchbook, or a billboard. Words are all you have. Words drive. Don't cut corners here. Your ad needs to tantalize, surprise, and entice. However, be wary of flooding the engine. A bloated ad trying to cover too many things in too little time is like driving in zig-zags. Yes, you're going forward...but not by much. Sacrifice trying to say it all in favor of something tight and clear.

Just Do It®

See? You can accomplish quite a bit without saying much.

And for goodness sake, let me enjoy the scenery.

"Entertainment is the currency that will purchase the attention of your customer."

– Roy H. Williams, Wizard of Ads

Now let's get you to Milwaukee (And no changing the destination in the middle of the trip. I promise you will run out of gas).

CHAPTER 27

HOW TO TALK TO MILLENNIALS

"But how do I reach the millennials?" That's THE marketing question of the past 5 years. You MUST talk to the millennials. But how?

I will now share with you a technique that cannot fail. It is the only way to talk to millennials so they will listen, become engaged, and become your customer.

The way you talk to millennials is...

like anyone else.

The latest research on millennials suggests that they are people. Your experiences may be different, but there is scientific data to back that up. As recently as November 2017, psychologists from Yale released a peer-reviewed report that has rocked the marketing industry. "After a 5-year study of 18,129 millennials," writes Dr. Margaret Sklar, Adjunct Professor of Neurology, "we concluded that 100% of them are people, with a margin of error +/- 3%"

We can infer from this that these "people," as Dr. Sklar calls them, have lives and motivations similar to humans. Even more staggering is how this parallels Dr. Maslow's Hierarchy of Human Needs.

"Human nature hasn't changed for a million years. It won't change in the next million years. Only the superficial things have changed. It's fashionable to talk about the changing man.

A communicator must be concerned with the unchanging man – what compulsions drive him, what instincts dominate his every action, even though his language too often camouflages what really motivates him."

– Bill Bernbach, legendary adman, DDB Worldwide

Let's back up a bit. Millennials are not a "market" to "target." There are 81 million of them in the U.S. That's not a market segment. That's enough to fill Denmark, Hong Kong, and Canada with room leftover for Australia and three Jamaicas. The idea that they all walk, talk, think, shop, and act en masse is no more plausible than suggesting the people of all those countries are the "same."

That's what Bernbach was getting at in that quote. "Millennials" are not a freak mutation doing "everything" differently. They are people. Just like Gen X, Gen Y, yuppies, hippies, and baby boomers. They go to work, they fall in love, they die, they cry, they have babies, and they invent new things. Some may spend the rest of their lives waiting tables, others will be Mark Zuckerberg, and every other combination in between.

They worry and laugh. They're irresponsible and brilliant. They wear shoes and buy cars. They enjoy ice cream cones and a nice salmon. Sometimes they're online, and then they are not. They get irrational and are open minded. They put on sweaters when they are cold and go swimming in the summer. They make art, make science, and make love.

We are more alike than we are different. The motivations of millennials are statistically equal to that of the pilgrims.

Talk to them like people. Because they are. The stuff on the surface may appear different, but the stuff in our hearts hasn't changed for a million years.

Maslow's Hierarchy of Human Needs gets batted around in advertising as much as Rosser Reeves' *Unique Selling Proposition.* And is as equally misunderstood. Dr. Abraham Maslow introduced his hierarchy in his paper "A Theory of Human Motivation." He didn't write it for marketers. It's a guide for psychologists, psychiatrists, and physicians. But it's useful in advertising because it outlines our purest motivations. We yearn for safety and belonging. We need love and family. We are curious and long to leave a legacy.

These are not the only human needs, but they can act as a map when you are trying to discover what motivates people to do what they do. They are flawlessly universal. Dr. M. listed them in order starting from our most basic. You can't go to the next one until you've fulfilled the first.

Physiological: Air, food, and water.

Safety: Is my food, family, and life safe?

Love/belonging: The need for family and friends.

Esteem: Confidence, self-esteem, and achievement.

Self-actualization: Morality, creativity, and problem solving.

CHAPTER 28

DECEMBER 31 6:43 P.M.

When I'm asked when a new ad campaign will start working, my answer is always December 31st, 6:43 PM.

January 1st

Your campaign is born.

March 18th

New customers are getting to know you. You aren't strangers, but you aren't going out for coffee either.

May 7th

Of the customers who are getting to know you, about 31% find you somewhat interesting. You just might have what they need.

August 3rd

Congratulations. You've made it onto a customer's mental list. You are now an option. Not the only option, but you've got a shot.

October 12th

You've got this customer convinced that your product/service is the right one *when the time comes*.

December 31st, 6:43 PM

Your advertising campaign is starting to work.

Your dates may vary. If yours is a product or service needed infrequently (plumbing, banking, mattresses, attorneys), this will likely take longer. But it never happens sooner. Your ad campaign is like a waltz: A polite introduction. Shy flirting. Awkward steps. If you pass that test, you may get a second date. Hopefully a 7th. It's a process everyone goes through, whether it's a friend, a business proposition, or a new lover. Nobody ever goes from "nice to meet ya" and jumps straight to "how about a weekend in Lake Tahoe?"

Your ad campaign will take a similar path, and there are some other dates you need to be aware of:

June 14th

Unexpected competitor opens a new location.

September 3rd

New legislation has changed how people buy your product.

November 21st

Your key employee passes away.

You will get bumped and bruised along the way. But the longer you stay with it, and the more focused you are, it gets better and easier. After 4 or 5 years of this, you can't wait for the next round of new people to discover you. You understand that they will also go through the steps of getting to know you. Plant the seeds and wait.

Is there a quicker way to do this? Sure. It's just not very pretty. You have to sacrifice your profits, principles, and pride. You'll need to bark as loud as possible and rent an inflatable-wiggly-arm-guy. You'll need to work twice as hard for half the margin. That will get you through January. Then you'll need to do it again in February. And March. And twice in April. And three times in May.

Be steady. Be deliberate. Be remarkable. Be patient. Be brave.

CHAPTER 29

ALWAYS PAY THE BUSKER

A busker gets up in the morning with one mission: make something remarkable. Ya gotta love that. Well, you don't "gotta," but you oughta.

Seth Godin has written a few times about the similarities between a busker and a business. Both are offering something of value that you will, hopefully, find interesting enough to pay money for. Therein is your challenge. Did you get up this morning and produce something so remarkable that it will stop people from walking past you?

The similarities between busking and business

sometimes get missed because it implies the only way to gain attention is by being a street performer or artist. It suggests that you must be "out there" and do something utterly original, even unorthodox. Advertisers then fling themselves out of orbit and become the "zany-screaming-mattress-guy" or the "I've-lost-my-mind-car-dealer." Woah, horse. Woah.

The goal is not to knock people out of their seats with a pie to the face and splash them with seltzer water (despite how hilarious that would be). The goal, regardless of your business, is to make your thing more interesting than the other person's thing.

The rub, as the busker knows too well, is that some people aren't interested. That's okay. You'll never get them all, and you don't have the capacity to handle them all even if you did. What you want is something that is special and meaningful to someone. It should be remarkable. People must remark about what you did for them. One becomes two. Two become four.

Accountants, chiropractors, car dealers, and roofers all need a little busker in them. It's an obligation to offer something, anything, that an accountant just like you doesn't (or can't) offer. An unexpected 13th donut from the baker. The "I'll be on time or you don't pay" plumber. A painter who can paint your home before you get home from work.

Are you offering something people will talk about?

Something they will need to talk about. Something meaningful to the customer that the mope down the street selling the same thing *will not do.*

If you see a street performer today, pay the busker. Because on that corner, at that time, the busker did something that caught your attention and was meaningful to you.

Pay the busker for the lesson you were just given.

CHAPTER 30

HARVEY JUMPED OFF A BRIDGE

"Damnit!"

It's customary to begin a phone conversation with "hello, how ya doin?" but Diane Barnes wasn't having it. She just saw an ad from her competitor, and it was causing her slight irritation. And by "slight" I mean a "*hornet sting*," and by "irritation" I mean "*on someone deathly allergic to hornet stings.*" Diane is competitive.

"Meyer has an ad in the paper about their anniversary charm bracelets."

"OK."

"We have those! Drives me crazy. People need to know we have those too."

Diane firmly believed Harvey Meyer and Sons Jewelry was the main competition of Barnes Jewelers. They're both about the same size and probably have about the same size share of the market. But that's where the similarities end. The position of each store was clearly different. Barnes excelled at colored gemstones. Rubies, emeralds, topaz, and the like. Meyer and Sons wasn't known for much of anything. Fuzzy and fumbling advertising scattered them all over the place.

"Those are customers who could be shopping here!"

"Yes, they certainly could. They could also be going to one of seven other places in town. Or, no place at all."

"Meyer drives me crazy."

While it's important to keep an eye on your competition, it's not useful to react every time they make a move.

"Diane, Meyer's ad doesn't mean that he's *getting* those customers. It just means he's running an ad."

"I know. I know. We talked about that."

An informal survey in town showed Barnes Jewelry was, without exception, the leader when it comes to colored gemstones. Meyer and Sons was known for discount jewelry. They would pop up around Mother's

Day, again at Christmas, and once more on Valentine's Day. Each time with a "blowout sale" of some sort. "Save 70%!" "Prices have never been lower."

The only fight against low prices is...lower prices. Somebody is going out of business with that strategy. The other play is to do nothing.

"Nothing," Diane said, with her typical skepticism.

"Diane, your mountain is the colored gemstones mountain. Right now, it's all yours. Nobody around you for as far as the eye can see."

"But..."

"Even Meyer. He doesn't know what he is, and the longer he keeps it that way, the better it is for you. If somebody starts sniffing around the colored gemstone mountain, you defend it. But just because Harvey is jumping off a bridge..."

"Yes, Mother. That doesn't mean I should too," Diane said, knowing she was getting worked up over nothing.

This isn't easy to do. As a business owner, you are hyper aware of what your competition is doing. But if you try to zig each time your competition zags, you're going to run out of energy and resources. Once you have claimed your position, defend it with all your might. But don't leave your position to go fight another battle.

CHAPTER 31

THE NON-EXISTENT MARKETING FORMULA

The messy truth of marketing is this: If there were a formula, everyone would be using it. You would simply plug numbers into a spreadsheet and *poof,* you have a formula. The marketing line in your budget often confounds accountants for this reason. How can you spend money and not know the exact return on your investment?

Welcome to the intersection of faith and fact. The blurry line between finesse and solidity. Poets and quants.

The world is fuzzy. The factors that will impact your marketing are almost infinite:

- Did it rain on the day of your sale?

- Did a competitor suddenly start a massive ad campaign?

- Did 60 Minutes do an exposé on fraud in your industry?

- Did your receptionist honk-off a good customer (the one who knows everybody)?

- Did your logoed truck run a red light and almost take out a school bus?

- Did a tree grow over your sign so nobody can see it from the road?

Fuzzy. And yeah, it does matter. Every business is as unique as a fingerprint. And every marketplace is just as different. But certain things are in your control:

- Know your customer

- Have a strategy

- Have a tight, bold message

- Be nimble, but do not veer off course

- Clean your restroom (freakishly more important than you might think)

- Stay out of the mud

- **Know your customer.** Climb around in their hearts

- Speak like a warm person, not a chilly business

Be ready to mix the qualitative and the quantitative. Too much of one is poison.

I cannot tell you to "take two aspirin and call me in the morning." That usually works...but then again, who knows? I can tell you to eat your fruits and vegetables. I know roughly how many calories you might need. Too much booze will kill you, but a glass of wine in the evening is probably fine.

I don't know if you'll win. But I believe you have an amazing story to tell...and I think you should tell it.

EPILOGUE AS A PROLOGUE

Advertising, comes from the 12th century the Latin word *advertere*, meaning "to turn toward," and from the 15th century Old French word *advertiss*, which means "make aware, call attention, remark." For most of advertising's history, simply making customers "aware" was plenty. Today, we are all from Missouri: "Show me. Prove it. Persuade me." Just "getting your name out there" won't get you to the mountaintop. I have the honor to have a group of business partners who believe in bold strategies and elegant writing. We believe in courageous local businesses, and that local businesses have the ability to grow big.

It's easy to critique advertising. It's even easier to hate it. We are constantly surrounded by it. We worry its abuse may alter presidential elections. We fear smart devices are listening to our private conversations about getting the laundry done, just to throw a Tide coupon at us at the exact moment we reach for the box.

Fairfax Cone (Foote, Cone & Belding, Chicago) tells us,

"Advertising is what you do when you can't go see somebody. That's all it is." Mr. Cone's quote is as true now as it was in the first half of the 1900s. There's not enough time in the day, and you can't hire enough salespeople, to go see everyone. If you want to invite people to your business, you do it in the form of advertising. If you want your business to hold a unique place in the minds of consumers, you do that with marketing.

We have a nearly uncountable amount of ways to advertise, but there is still only **one** way to market. I hope you sensed the important difference between the two while reading this.

You absolutely can do this yourself, and for some businesses, you have no choice. While you *can* do it yourself, I believe finding somebody you trust to keep an unbiased eye on your brand and brand promise is crucial. To work, sweat, and bleed building a company, only to have it collapse because somebody betrayed your principles is heartbreaking. Sometimes you, the business owner, get so deep in the "busy-ness" of running your business, you get confused and fumble it yourself.

It's not easy to gain the trust of a skeptical consumer. It takes almost nothing violate that trust. Regaining trust can be like raising the Titanic.

I sat down to write this book because I believe in you. The freakish courage it takes to start a business baffles me. It really does. I also know marketing takes freakish courage. "Marketing" began the moment you said, "I think I'll open a store."

You're already marketing your business, even if marketing doesn't interest you at all. Minus marketing, you're driving a car missing a wheel.

I hope you give it some serious thought, because marketing is the silent force that makes this whole megillah work.

I DID IT! THREE MEGILLAHS IN ONE BOOK!

Good luck. God Speed. Be careful out there.

RESOURCES

In no particular order, here are some fine books and other resources you may find helpful:

The Wizard of Ads
Secret Formulas of the Wizard of Ads
Magical Worlds of the Wizard of Ads
Roy H. Williams

Positioning: The Battle for Your Mind
The 22 Immutable Laws of Marketing
Al Ries and Jack Trout

Selling the Invisible: A Field Guide to Modern Marketing
Harry Beckwith

Brandsformation: How to Transform a Good Local Business into a Great Brand
Chuck Mefford

Be Like Amazon: Even a Lemonade Stand Can Do It
Waiting for Your Cat to Bark? Persuading Customers When They Ignore Marketing
Jeffrey Eisenberg and Bryan Eisenberg

Influence: The Psychology of Persuasion
Pre-Suasion: Channeling Attention for Change
Dr. Robert Cialdini

Yes! 50 Scientifically Proven Ways to Be Persuasive
Noah J. Goldstein, Steve J. Martin, and Robert B. Cialdini

Start with Why: How Great Leaders Inspire Everyone to Take Action
Simon Sinek

All Marketers are Liars: The Power of Telling Authentic Stories in a Low-Trust World
Purple Cow: Transform Your Business by Being Remarkable
Permission Marketing: Turning Strangers into Friends and Friends into Customers
Seth Godin

Ogilvy On Advertising
Confessions of an Ad Man
David Ogilvy

Brand Your Own Business: A Step-by-Step Guide to Being Known, Liked, and Trusted in the Age of Rapid Distraction
Tim Miles and Ryan Patrick

Made to Stick: Why Some Ideas Survive and Others Die
Chip Heath and Dan Heath

The Strategy Wizard: How to Make Lovable Local Marketing for Bonk'n Good Business
Michael D. Slover

Donoricity: Raise More Money for Your Nonprofit with Strategies Your Donors Crave
Steve Thomas

Strategy Daddy: Marketing Strategies, Tactics and Case Studies That Can Change the Competitive Landscape of Your Business
Michael Keesee and Ankesh Kothari

Fishing for Customers and Reeling Them In
Chuck McKay

...plus any number of books, podcasts, and articles written by the always prolific Wizard of Ads partners (www.wizardofads.com). I'm certain I missed several.

You can get astounding help from any of our partners at Wizard of Ads. There's not-a-one I wouldn't trust with your business (or mine).

You can find me at:
www.disruptingads.com
johnny@disruptingads.com

FIN
BUT WAIT!
THERE'S MORE!

The tome you just finished is comprised of stories that have actually happened to people who don't actually exist. How businesses conduct themselves is personal and private. One of my core principles is to honor the confidentiality of the businesses who hire me. Another core principle of mine is that each business has its own DNA. To copy marketing strategies from one business and try to force-fit those strategies onto another would be both ineffective and unethical.

Be true to the honesty of your business' pure, true character. Reject the temptation to apply the tactics and techniques that helped a plumber in Poughkeepsie succeed. Unless you are that exact plumber in Poughkeepsie, it will not work as strongly and as magically as it could.

CPSIA information can be obtained
at www.ICGtesting.com
Printed in the USA
LVHW080046120419
613893LV00002B/2/P